EASY GUITAR
WITH NOTES & TAB

BEST OF ANTONIO CARLOS JOBIM

Cover photo by Michael Ochs Archives / Getty Images

ISBN 978-1-4234-3430-6

HAL•LEONARD®
CORPORATION

7777 W. BLUEMOUND RD. P.O. BOX 13819 MILWAUKEE, WI 53213

Visit Hal Leonard Online at
www.halleonard.com

STRUM AND PICK PATTERNS

This chart contains the suggested strum and pick patterns that are referred to by number at the beginning of each song in this book. The symbols ⊓ and ∨ in the strum patterns refer to down and up strokes, respectively. The letters in the pick patterns indicate which right-hand fingers plays which strings.

p = thumb
i = index finger
m = middle finger
a = ring finger

For example; Pick Pattern 2
is played: thumb - index - middle - ring

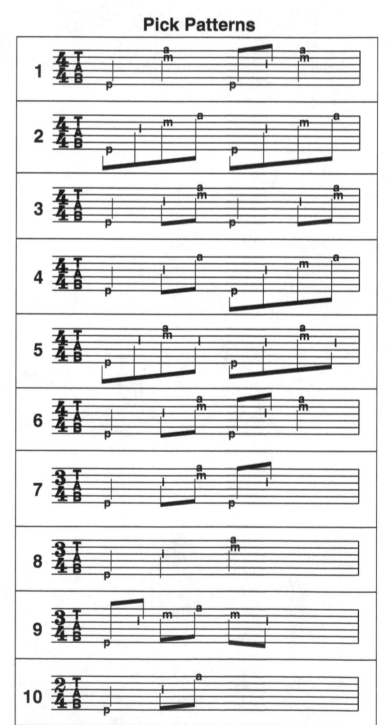

Strum Patterns   **Pick Patterns**

You can use the 3/4 Strum or Pick Patterns in songs written in compound meter (6/8, 9/8, 12/8, etc.).
For example, you can accompany a song in 6/8 by playing the 3/4 pattern twice in each measure.
The 4/4 Strum and Pick Patterns can be used for songs written in cut time (¢) by doubling the note
time values in the patterns. Each pattern would therefore last two measures in cut time.

Desafinado
(Off Key)

English Lyric by Gene Lees
Original Text by Newton Mendonca
Music by Antonio Carlos Jobim

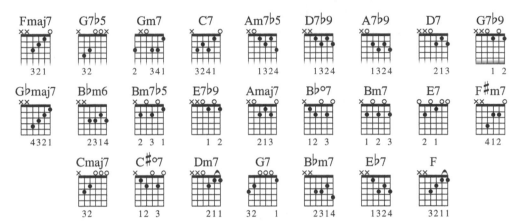

Strum Pattern: 3
Pick Pattern: 3

Verse
Moderate Bossa

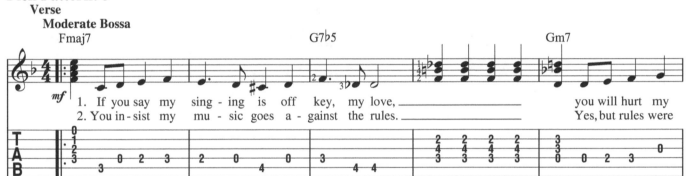

1. If you say my sing-ing is off key, my love, _____ you will hurt my
2. You in-sist my mu-sic goes a-gainst the rules. _____ Yes, but rules were

feel-ings, don't you see, my love? _____ I wish I had an ear like yours, a voice that would be-
nev-er made for love-sick fools; _____

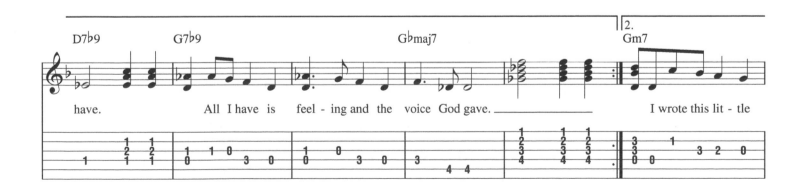

have. All I have is feel-ing and the voice God gave. _____ I wrote this lit-tle

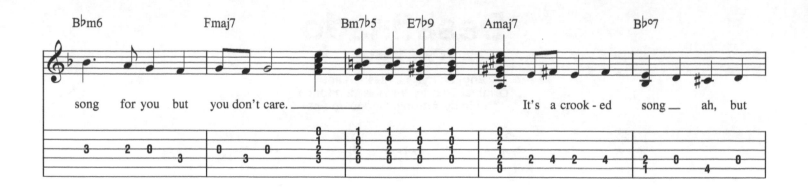

song   for you but   you don't care._____   It's a crook - ed   song __ ah, but

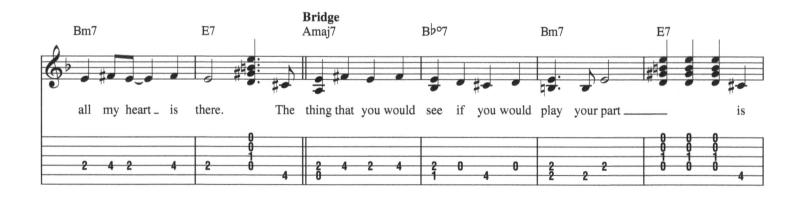

all   my heart _ is   there.   The thing that you would see if you would play   your part _____   is

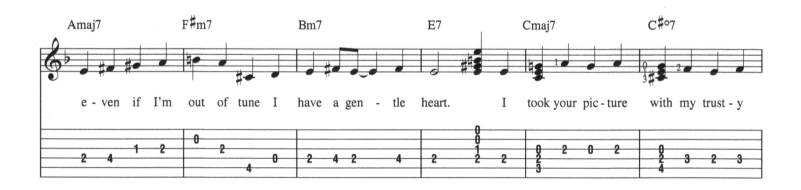

e - ven if I'm out of tune I have a gen - tle heart.   I   took your pic - ture   with my trust - y

Rol - lei - flex. _____   and now   all   I have de - vel - oped is a   com - plex. _____

Verse

3. Pos-si-bly in vain I hope you weak-en, oh — my love. _____ And for-get those

rig - id rules that un-der-mine my dream of a life of love and mu - sic with some - one who'll un-der-

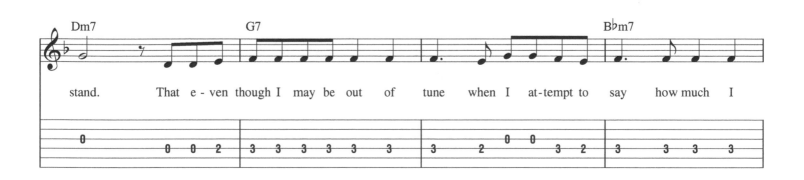

stand. That e - ven though I may be out of tune when I at-tempt to say how much I

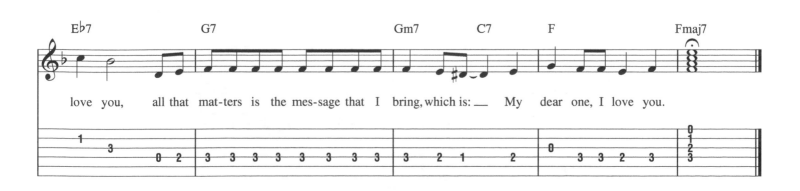

love you, all that mat-ters is the mes-sage that I bring, which is: — My dear one, I love you.

Água de Beber
(Water to Drink)

English Words by Norman Gimbel
Portuguese Words by Vinicius De Moraes
Music by Antonio Carlos Jobim

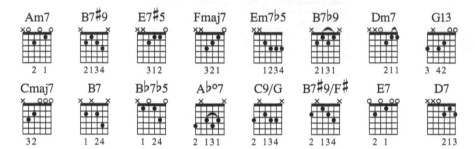

Strum Pattern: 3
Pick Pattern: 1

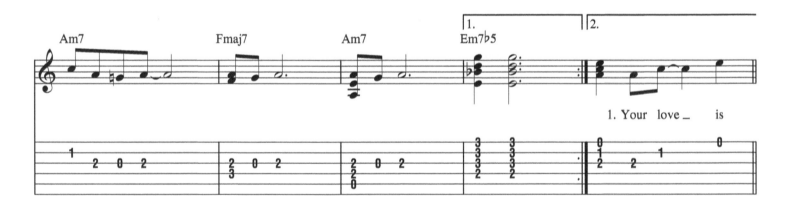

1. Your love _ is

rain, my heart the flow-er. _____ I need _ your love or I will die.

2. *See additional lyrics*

Additional Lyrics

2. The rain can fall on distant deserts.
   The rain can fall upon the sea.
   The rain can fall upon the flower.
   Since the rain has to fall, let it fall on me.

Aguas de Marco
(Waters of March)

Words and Music by Antonio Carlos Jobim

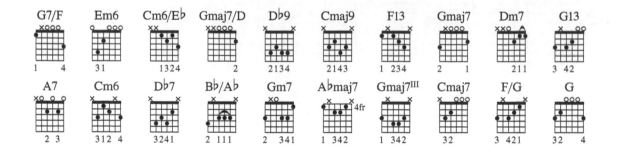

Strum Pattern: 3
Pick Pattern: 1, 3

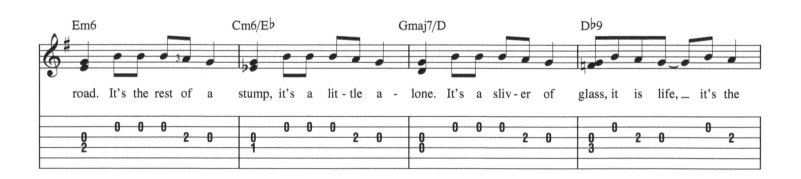

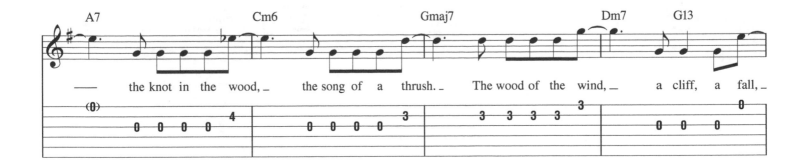

the knot in the wood, _ the song of a thrush. _ The wood of the wind, _ a cliff, a fall, _

_ a scratch, a lump, it is noth-ing at all. It's the wind blow-ing free, it's the end of the

slope, it's a beam, it's a void, it's a hunch, it's a hope, and the riv - er-bank talks of the Wa-ters of

Verse

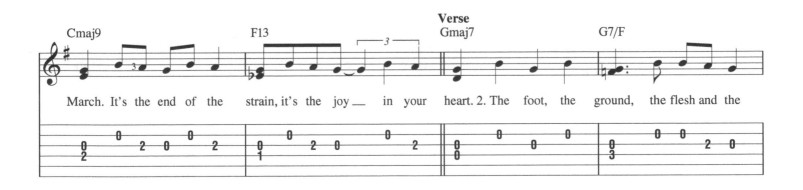

March. It's the end of the strain, it's the joy _ in your heart. 2. The foot, the ground, the flesh and the

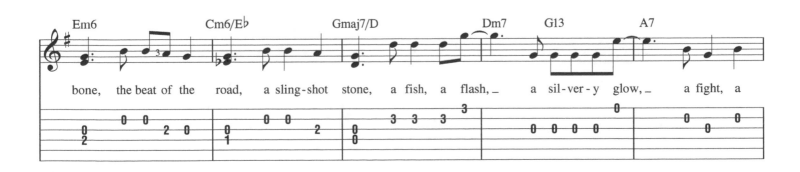

bone, the beat of the road, a sling-shot stone, a fish, a flash, _ a sil-ver-y glow, _ a fight, a

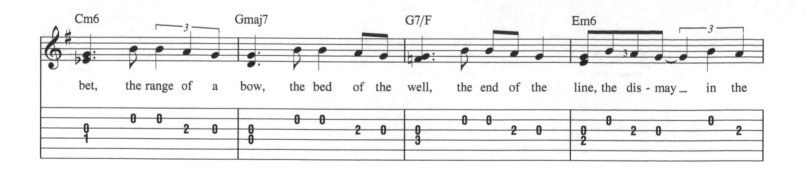

bet, the range of a bow, the bed of the well, the end of the line, the dis - may _ in the

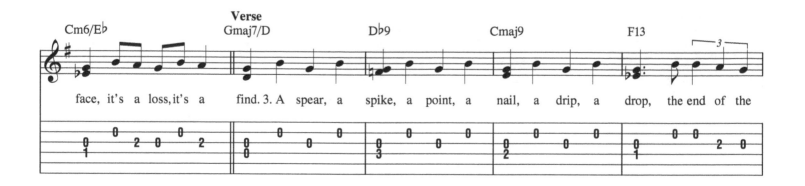

face, it's a loss, it's a find. 3. A spear, a spike, a point, a nail, a drip, a drop, the end of the

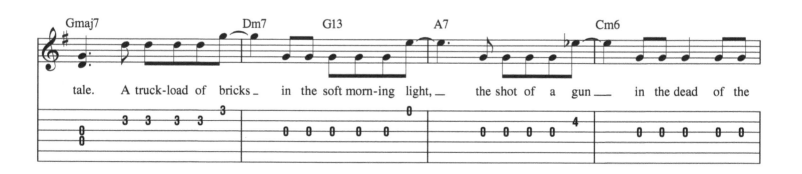

tale. A truck-load of bricks _ in the soft morn-ing light, _ the shot of a gun _ in the dead of the

night. A mile, _ a must, _ a thrust, _ a bump, _ it's a girl, _ it's a rhyme, it's a cold, _ it's the

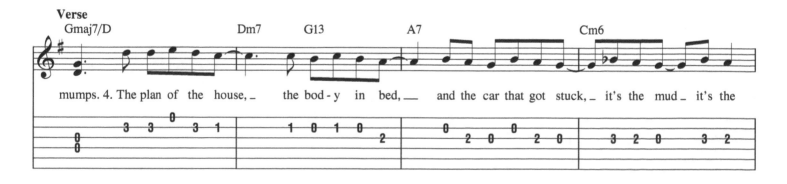

mumps. 4. The plan of the house, _ the bod - y in bed, _ and the car that got stuck, _ it's the mud _ it's the

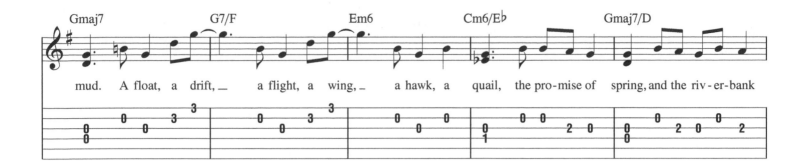

mud. A float, a drift, __ a flight, a wing, __ a hawk, a quail, the pro-mise of spring, and the riv-er-bank

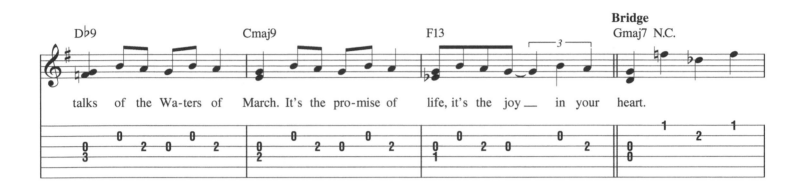

talks of the Wa-ters of March. It's the pro-mise of life, it's the joy __ in your heart.

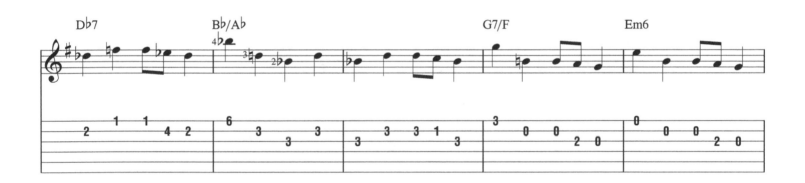

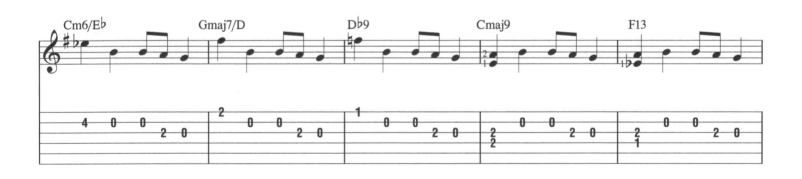

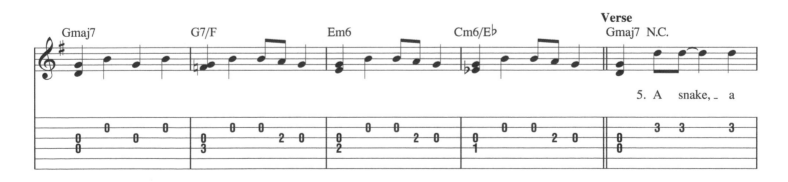

5. A snake, __ a

stick, it is John, it is Joe, it's a thorn in your hand, and a cut on your toe. A point, a grain, a bee, a

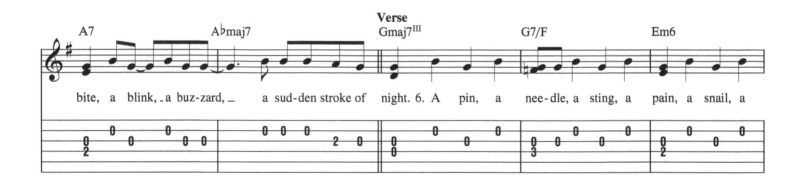

bite, a blink, a buz-zard, __ a sud-den stroke of night. 6. A pin, a nee-dle, a sting, a pain, a snail, a

Verse

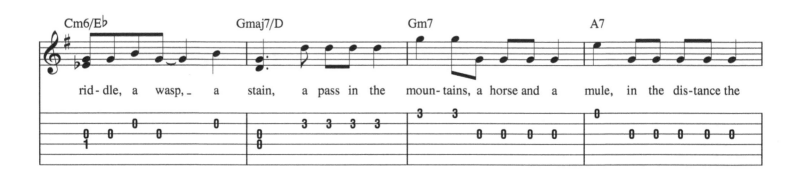

rid-dle, a wasp, __ a stain, a pass in the moun-tains, a horse and a mule, in the dis-tance the

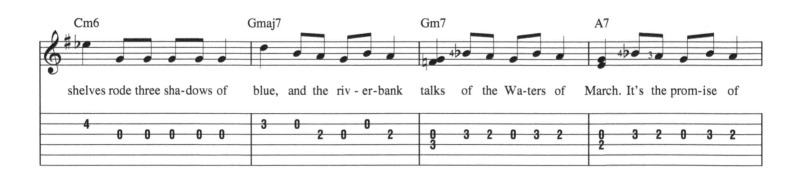

shelves rode three sha-dows of blue, and the riv-er-bank talks of the Wa-ters of March. It's the prom-ise of

Verse

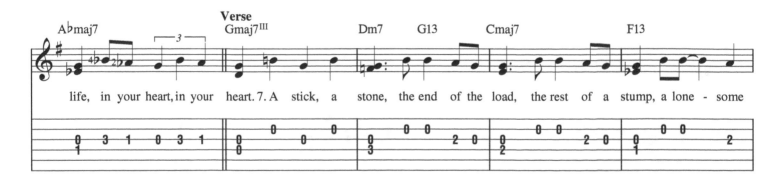

life, in your heart, in your heart. 7. A stick, a stone, the end of the load, the rest of a stump, a lone - some

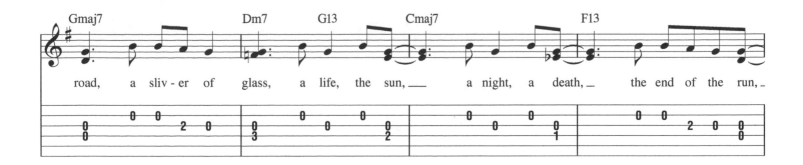

road,   a   sliv-er of   glass,   a   life,   the sun,   a   night, a death,   the   end of the run,

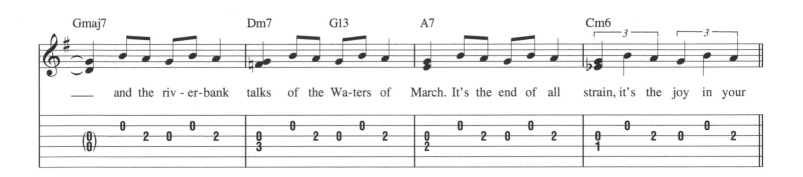

   and the riv-er-bank talks of the Wa-ters of   March. It's the end of all   strain, it's the joy in your

Outro

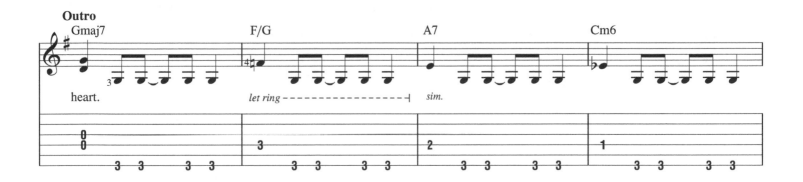

heart.   *let ring* - - - - - - - - - - - - - - - - - - *sim.*

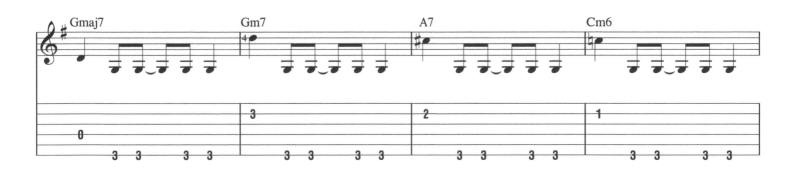

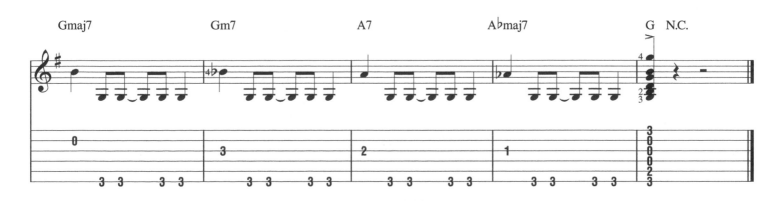

Dindi

Music by Antonio Carlos Jobim
Portuguese Lyrics by Aloysio de Oliveira
English Lyrics by Ray Gilbert

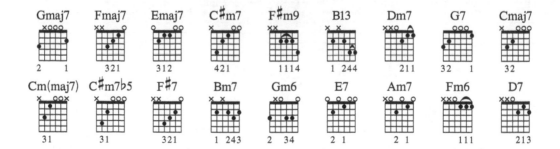

Strum Pattern: 4
Pick Pattern: 3

Verse
Freely

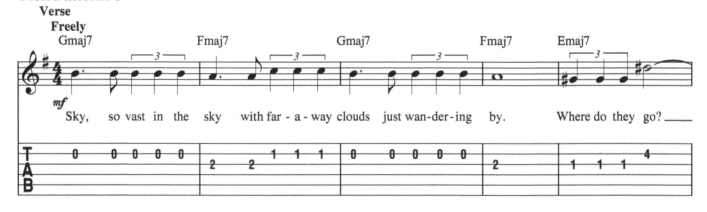

Sky, so vast in the sky with far-a-way clouds just wan-der-ing by. Where do they go?

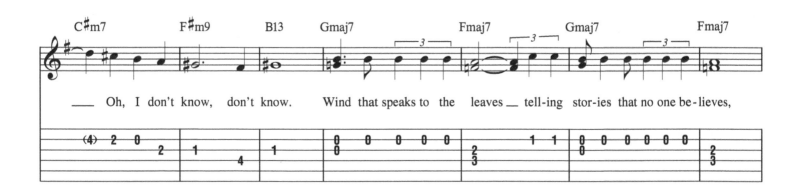

Oh, I don't know, don't know. Wind that speaks to the leaves tell-ing stor-ies that no one be-lieves,

Chorus
Moderate Bossa Nova

stor-ies of love be-long to you and me. Oh, Din-di, if I on-ly had words I would

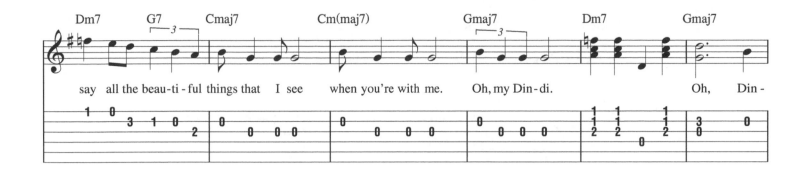

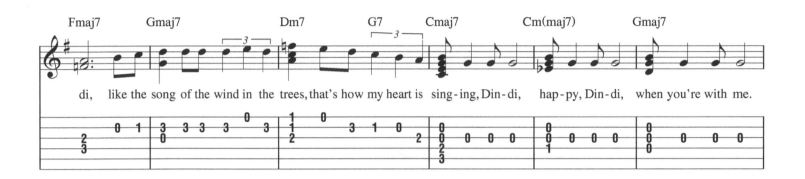

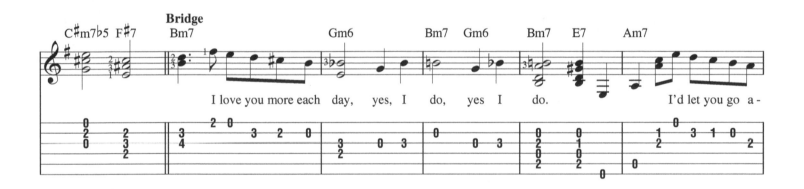

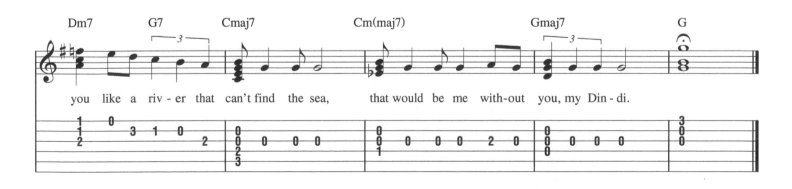

A Felicidade

Words and Music by Vinicius de Moraes, Andre Salvet and Antonio Carlos Jobim

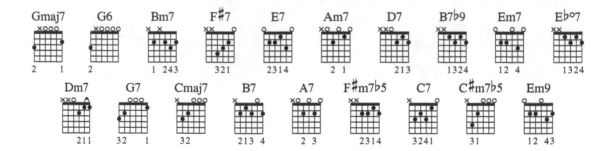

Strum Pattern: 3, 6
Pick Pattern: 1, 6

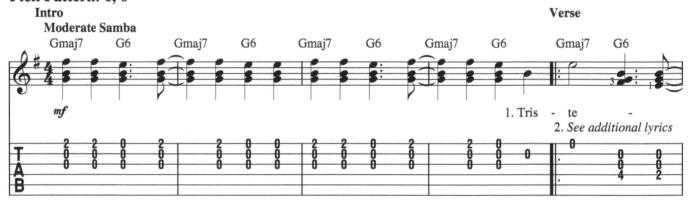

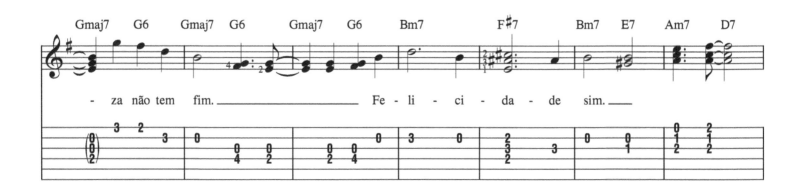

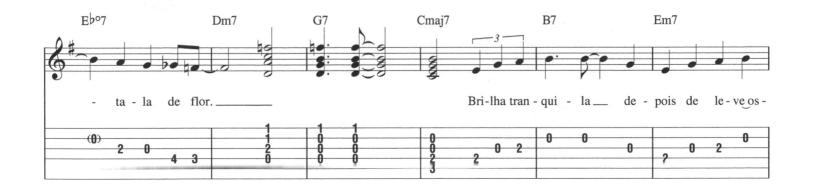

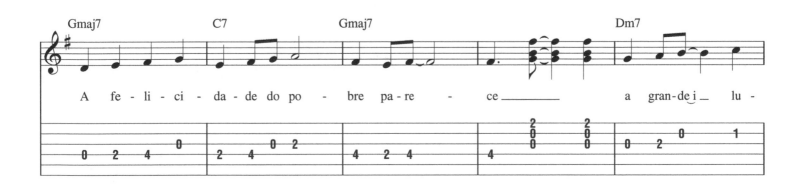

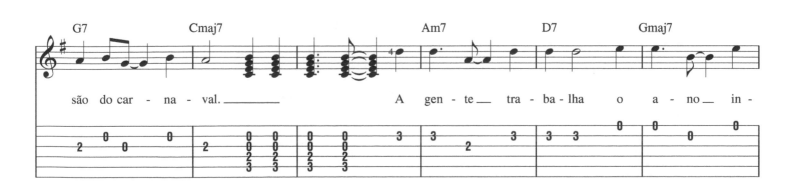

tei - ro   por   um   mo - men - to   de   son - ho ___ pra   fa - zer   a ___ fan - ta - si - a   de

rei   ou   de   pi - ra - ta ou jar - di - nei - ra. ___   E   tu - do se a - ca-

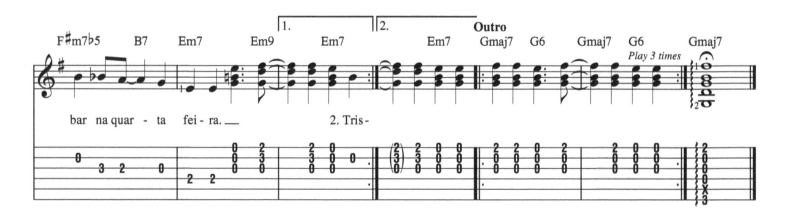

bar na quar - ta   fei - ra. ___   2. Tris-

Additional Lyrics

2. Tristeza não tem fim
   Felicidade sim.
   A felicidade é como a pluma
   Que ovento vai levando pelo ar.
   Voa tão leve mas tem a vida breve.
   Precisa que haja vento sem parar.
   A minha felicidade está sonhando
   Nos olhos da minha namorada.
   E como esta noite, passando, passando
   Em busca da madrugada.
   Falem baixo, por favor
   Prá que ela acorde alegre com o dia,
   Oferecendo beijos de amor.

The Girl from Ipanema

(Garôta de Ipanema)

Music by Antonio Carlos Jobim
English Words by Norman Gimbel
Original Words by Vinicius de Moraes

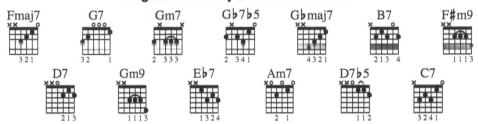

Strum Pattern: 3
Pick Pattern: 3

Verse

Moderate Bossa Nova

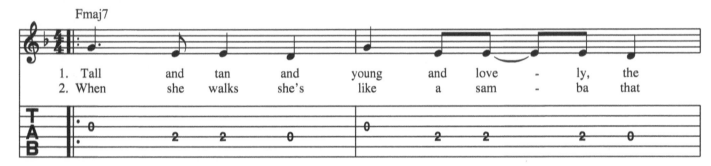

1. Tall and tan and young and love - ly, the
2. When she walks she's young like a sam - ba that

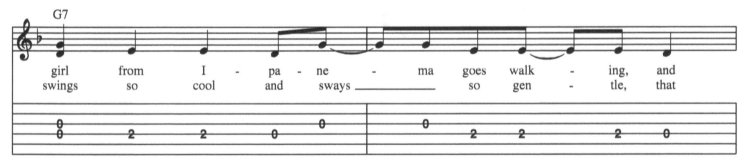

girl from I - pa - ne - ma goes walk - ing, and
swings so cool and sways _____ so gen - tle, that

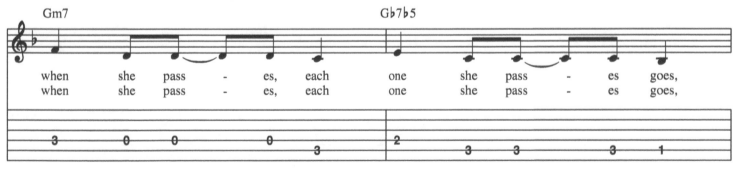

when she pass - es, each one she pass - es goes,
when she pass - es, each one she pass - es goes,

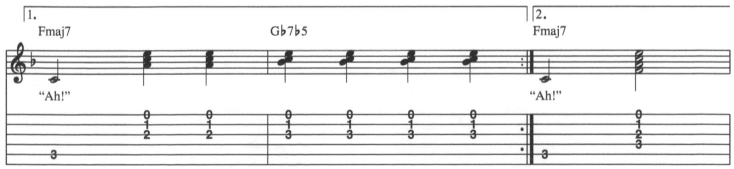

1.
"Ah!"

2.
"Ah!"

Bridge

How Insensitive
(Insensatez)

Music by Antonio Carlos Jobim
Original Words by Vinicius de Moraes
English Words by Norman Gimbel

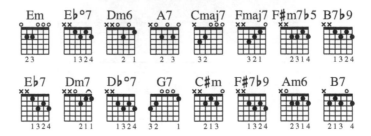

Strum Pattern: 3
Pick Pattern: 3

Verse
Moderate Bossa Nova

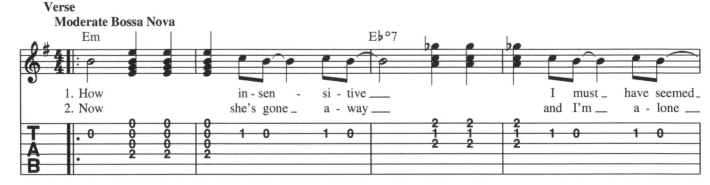

1. How in-sen-si-tive ___ I must ___ have seemed ___
2. Now she's gone ___ a-way ___ and I'm ___ a-lone ___

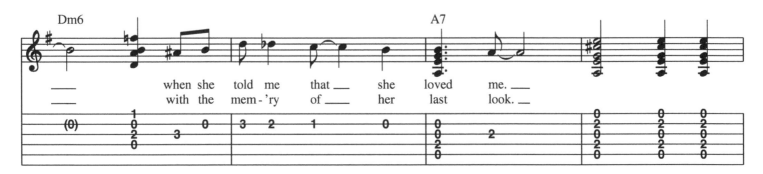

when she told me that ___ she loved me. ___
with the mem-'ry of ___ her last look. ___

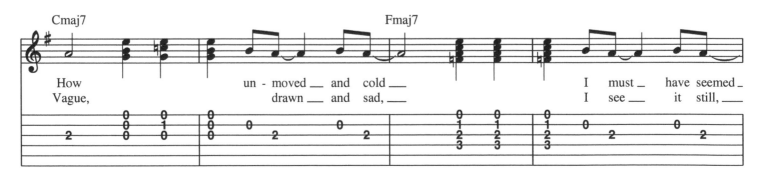

How un-moved ___ and cold ___ I must ___ have seemed ___
Vague, drawn ___ and sad, ___ I see ___ it still, ___

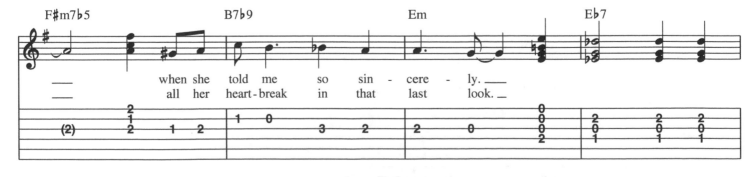

when she told me so sin-cere-ly. ___
all her heart-break in that last look. ___

Meditation
(Meditacão)

Music by Antonio Carlos Jobim
Original Words by Newton Mendonça
English Words by Norman Gimbel

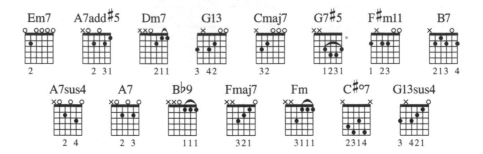

Strum Pattern: 3, 6
Pick Pattern: 1, 6

Intro
Moderate Bossa

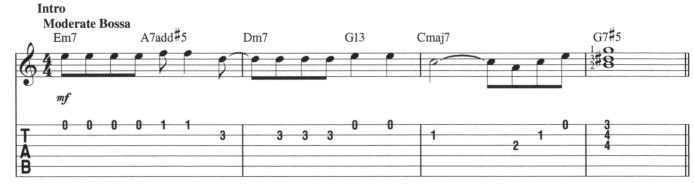

%: Verse

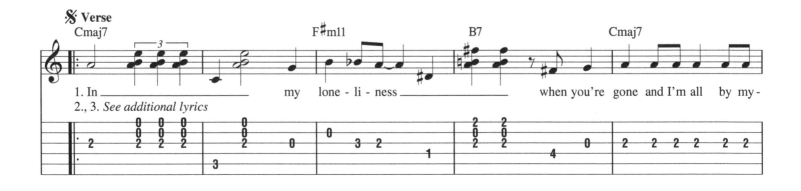

1. In _____ my lone‑li‑ness _____ when you're gone and I'm all by my‑
2., 3. *See additional lyrics*

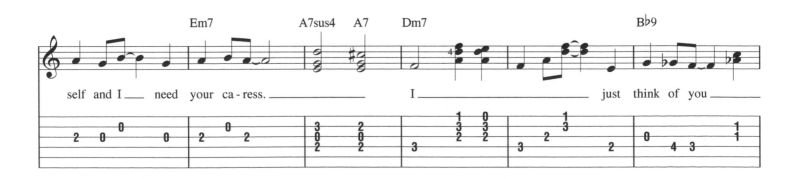

self and I __ need your ca‑ress. _____ I _____ just think of you __

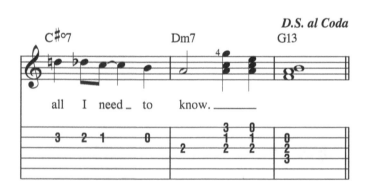
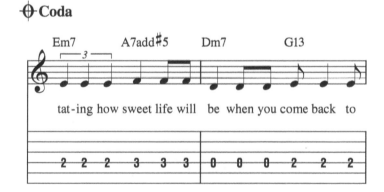

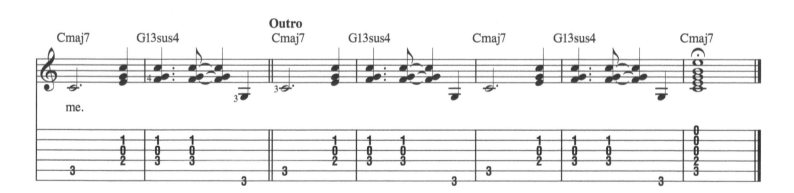

Additional Lyrics

2. Though you're far away,
   I have only to close my eyes and you are back to stay.
   I just close my eyes
   And the sadness that missing you brings
   Soon is gone and this heart of mine sings.

3. I will wait for you
   'Til the sun falls from out of the sky, for what else can I do?
   I will wait for you,
   Meditating how sweet life will be
   When you come back to me.

Once I Loved
(Amor em Paz) (Love in Peace)

Music by Antonio Carlos Jobim
Portuguese Lyrics by Vinicius de Moraes
English Lyrics by Ray Gilbert

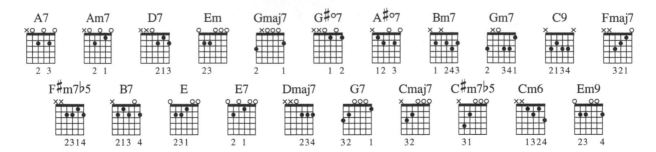

Strum Pattern: 4
Pick Pattern: 6, 1

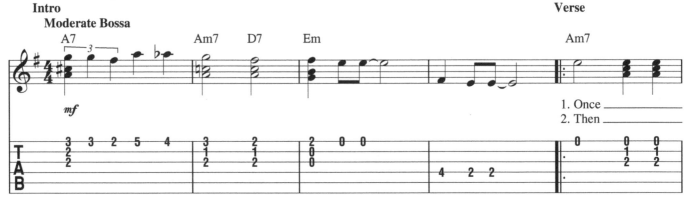

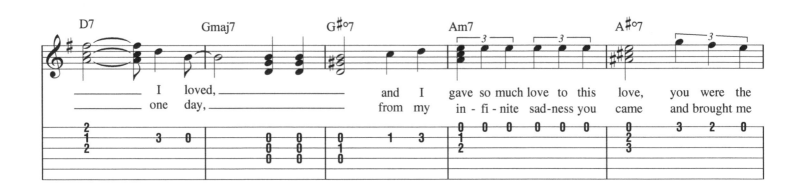

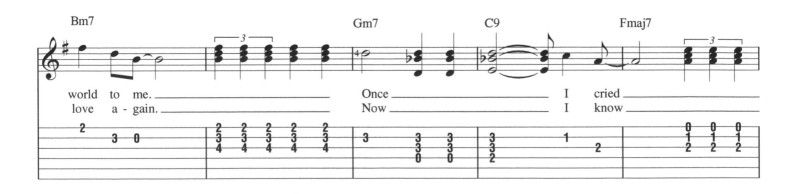

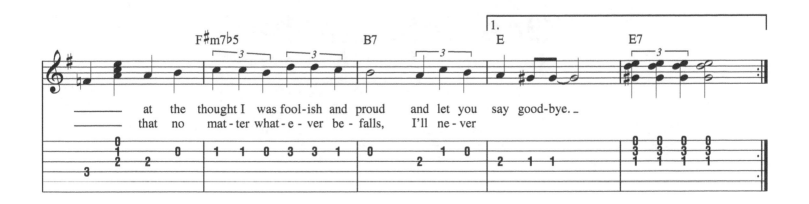

at the thought I was fool-ish and proud, and let you say good-bye.
that no mat-ter what-e-ver be-falls, I'll ne-ver

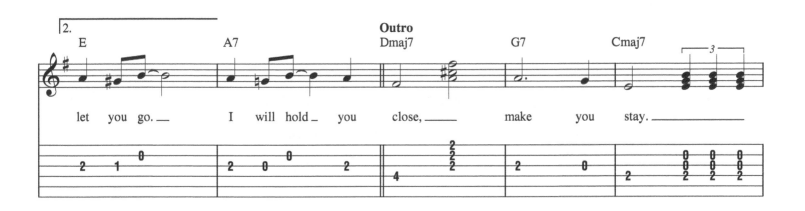

let you go. I will hold you close, make you stay.

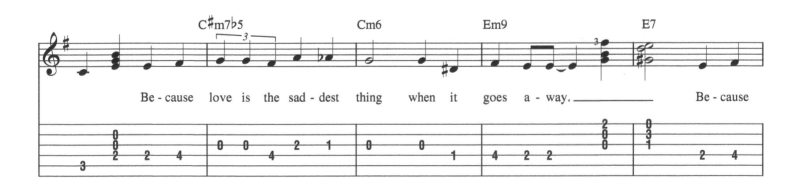

Be-cause love is the sad-dest thing when it goes a-way. Be-cause

love is the sad-dest thing when it goes a-way.

One Note Samba
(Samba de Uma Nota So)

Original Lyrics by Newton Mendonca
English Lyrics by Antonio Carlos Jobim
Music by Antonio Carlos Jobim

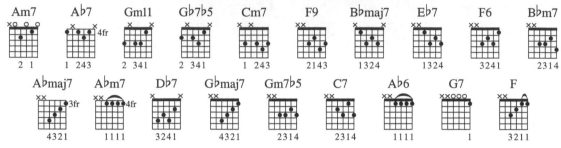

Strum Pattern: 3, 6
Pick Pattern: 1, 3

Verse
Moderate Bossa

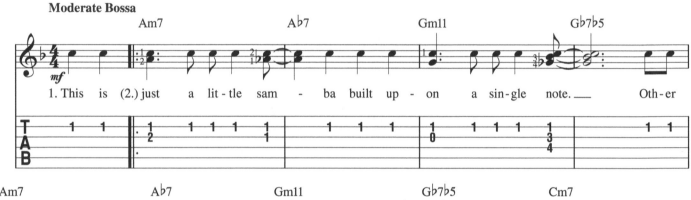

1. This is (2.) just a lit-tle sam-ba built up-on a sin-gle note. __ Oth-er

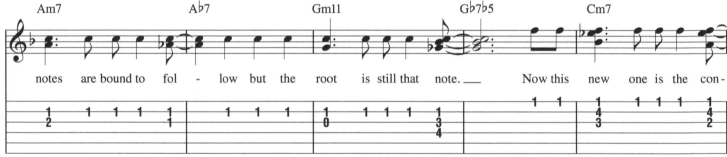

notes are bound to fol-low but the root is still that note. __ Now this new one is the con-

-se-quence of the one we've just been through, _ as I'm bound to be the un-a-void-a-ble

Bridge

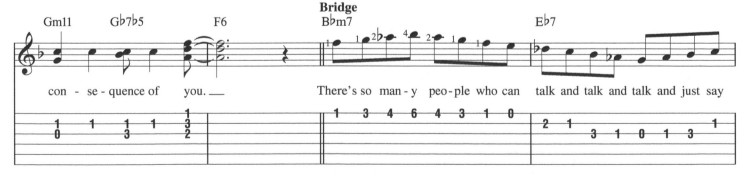

con-se-quence of you. __ There's so man-y peo-ple who can talk and talk and talk and just say

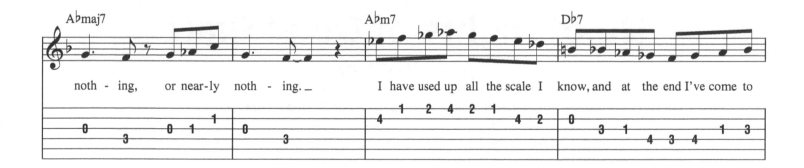

nothing, or near-ly noth - ing. __ I have used up all the scale I know, and at the end I've come to

Outro-Verse

nothing, or near-ly noth - ing. __ So I come back to my first __ note, as I

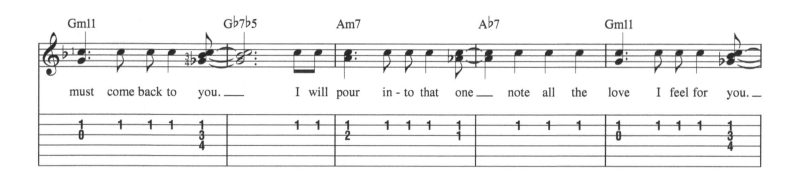

must come back to you. __ I will pour in-to that one __ note all the love I feel for you. __

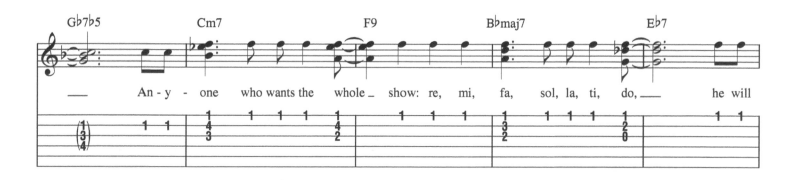

__ An-y-one who wants the whole __ show: re, mi, fa, sol, la, ti, do, __ he will

find him-self with no __ show. Bet-ter play the note you know. __ 2. This is __

Quiet Nights of Quiet Stars
(Corcovado)

English Words by Gene Lees
Original Words and Music by Antonio Carlos Jobim

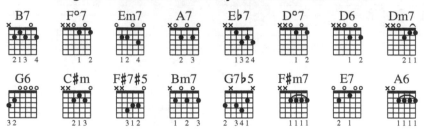

Strum Pattern: 4
Pick Pattern: 1, 6

Moderately slow

Qui - et nights of qui - et stars, _____ qui - et chords from my ___ gui - tar _____

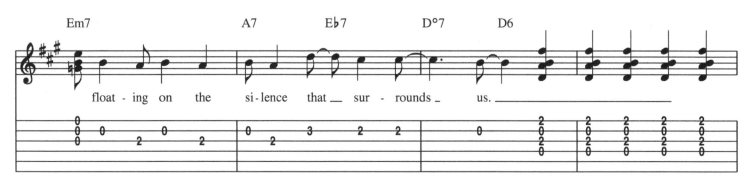

float - ing on the si - lence that ___ sur - rounds ___ us. _____

Qui - et thoughts and qui - et dreams, _____ qui - et walks by qui - et streams, _____

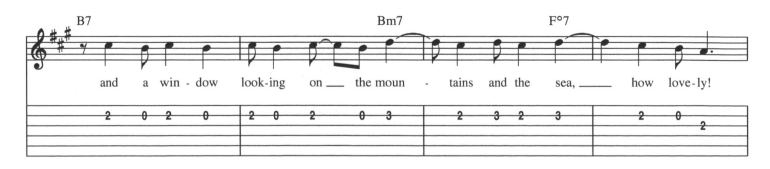

and a win - dow look - ing on ___ the moun - tains and the sea, _____ how love - ly!

This is where I want to be. _____ Here, with you so close to me ___ un - til ___

_____ the fi - nal flick - er of ___ life's em - ber. _____

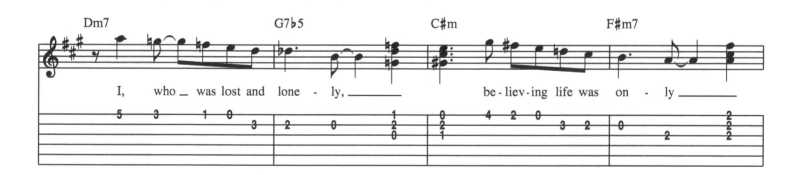

I, who ___ was lost and lone - ly, _____ be - liev - ing life was on - ly _____

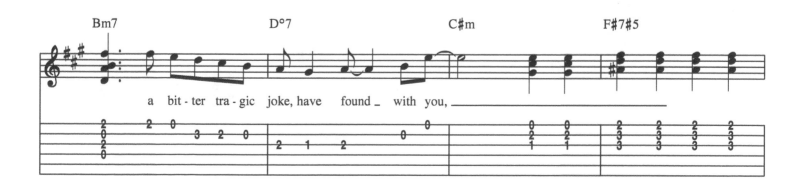

a bit - ter tra - gic joke, have found ___ with you, _____

the mean - ing of ex - ist - ence. Oh, ___ my love. _____

Só Danço Samba
(Jazz 'n' Samba)

English Lyric by Norman Gimbel
Original Text by Vinicius de Moraes
Music by Antonio Carlos Jobim

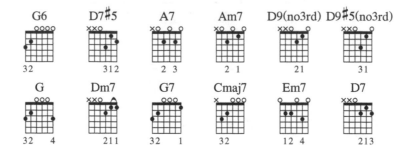

Strum Pattern: 6
Pick Pattern: 3, 4

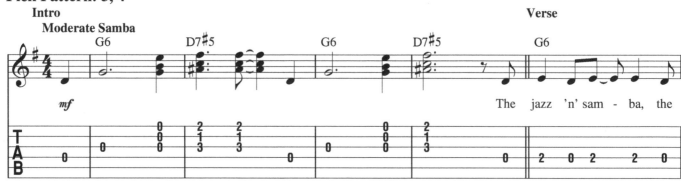

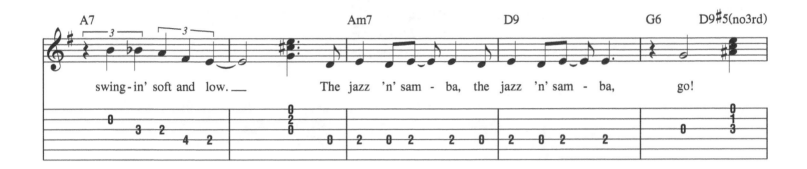

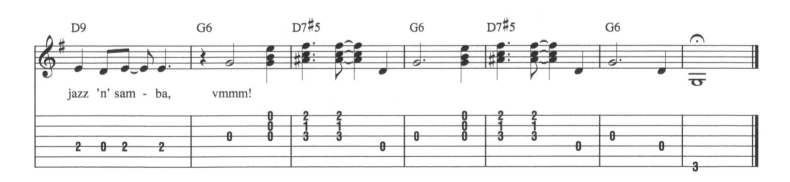

Triste

By Antonio Carlos Jobim

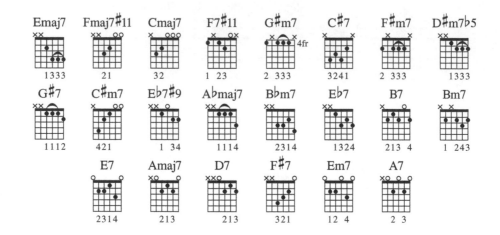

Strum Pattern: 2, 5
Pick Pattern: 4, 6

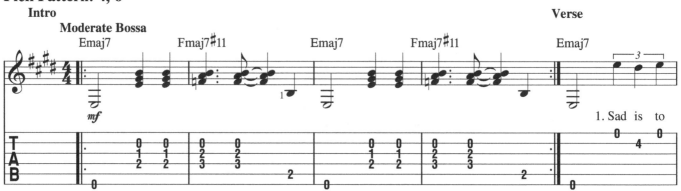

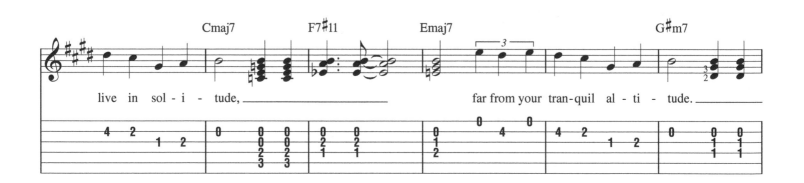

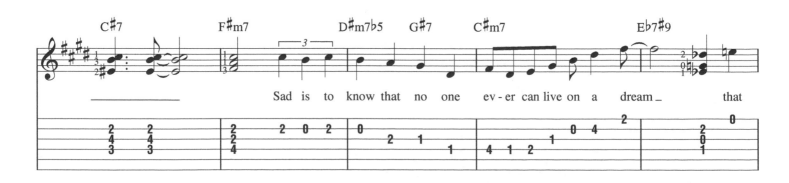

nev - er can be, __ will ne - ver be. __ Dream-er a - wake, __ wake up and see. __

Verse

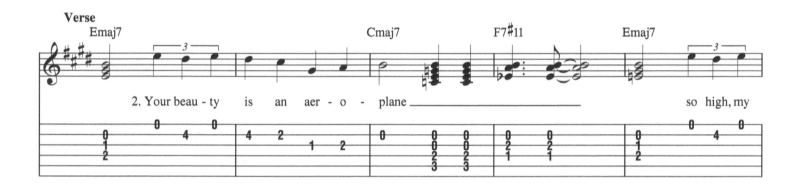

2. Your beau - ty is an aer - o - plane _____ so high, my

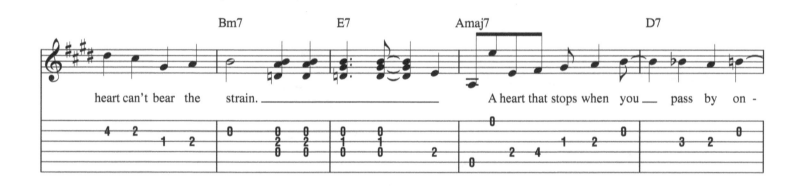

heart can't bear the strain. _____ A heart that stops when you __ pass by on -

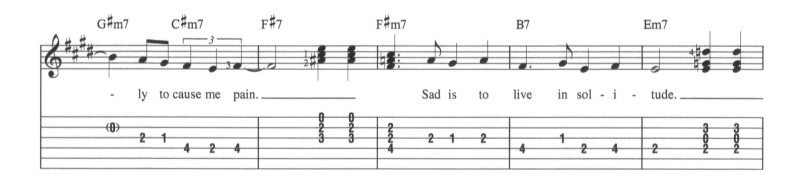

- ly to cause me pain. _____ Sad is to live in sol - i - tude. _____

Outro

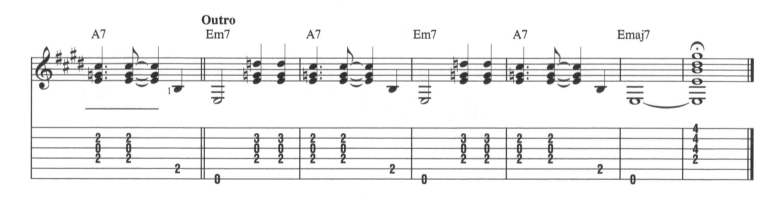

Wave

Words and Music by Antonio Carlos Jobim

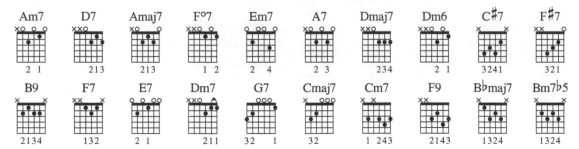

Strum Pattern: 3, 6
Pick Pattern: 4, 6

1. So close your eyes, ___ for

2. See additional lyrics

that's a love-ly way to be, _____ a-ware of things your heart ___ a - lone was meant to

see. _____ The fun-da-men - tal lone-li-ness goes ___ when-ev - er two can dream a dream to-geth-

- er. ___

2. You can't de -

When I saw you first, the time was half past three.

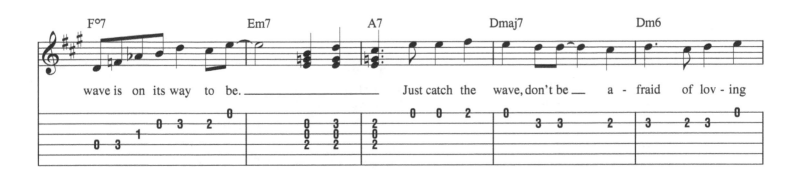

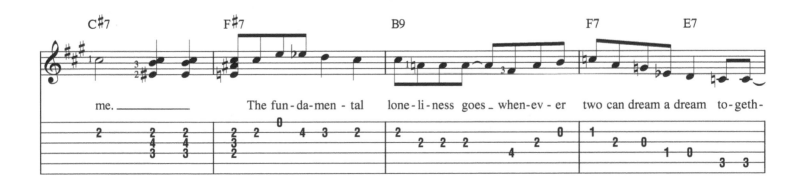

Additional Lyrics

2. You can't deny,
   Don't try to fight the rising sea.
   Don't fight the moon, the stars above,
   And don't fight me.
   The fundamental loneliness goes whenever
   Two can dream a dream together.

EASY GUITAR WITH NOTES & TAB

This series features simplified arrangements with notes, tab, chord charts, and strum and pick patterns.

MIXED FOLIOS

00702287	Acoustic	$19.99
00702002	Acoustic Rock Hits for Easy Guitar	$15.99
00702166	All-Time Best Guitar Collection	$19.99
00702232	Best Acoustic Songs for Easy Guitar	$16.99
00119835	Best Children's Songs	$16.99
00703055	The Big Book of Nursery Rhymes & Children's Songs	$16.99
00698978	Big Christmas Collection	$19.99
00702394	Bluegrass Songs for Easy Guitar	$15.99
00289632	Bohemian Rhapsody	$19.99
00703387	Celtic Classics	$16.99
00224808	Chart Hits of 2016-2017	$14.99
00267383	Chart Hits of 2017-2018	$14.99
00334293	Chart Hits of 2019-2020	$16.99
00403479	Chart Hits of 2021-2022	$16.99
00702149	Children's Christian Songbook	$9.99
00702028	Christmas Classics	$8.99
00101779	Christmas Guitar	$14.99
00702141	Classic Rock	$8.95
00159642	Classical Melodies	$12.99
00253933	Disney/Pixar's Coco	$16.99
00702203	CMT's 100 Greatest Country Songs	$34.99
00702283	The Contemporary Christian Collection	$16.99

00196954	Contemporary Disney	$19.99
00702239	Country Classics for Easy Guitar	$24.99
00702257	Easy Acoustic Guitar Songs	$17.99
00702041	Favorite Hymns for Easy Guitar	$12.99
00222701	Folk Pop Songs	$17.99
00126894	Frozen	$14.99
00333922	Frozen 2	$14.99
00702286	Glee	$16.99
00702160	The Great American Country Songbook	$19.99
00702148	Great American Gospel for Guitar	$14.99
00702050	Great Classical Themes for Easy Guitar	$9.99
00275088	The Greatest Showman	$17.99
00148030	Halloween Guitar Songs	$14.99
00702273	Irish Songs	$14.99
00192503	Jazz Classics for Easy Guitar	$16.99
00702275	Jazz Favorites for Easy Guitar	$17.99
00702274	Jazz Standards for Easy Guitar	$19.99
00702162	Jumbo Easy Guitar Songbook	$24.99
00232285	La La Land	$16.99
00702258	Legends of Rock	$14.99
00702189	MTV's 100 Greatest Pop Songs	$34.99
00702272	1950s Rock	$16.99
00702271	1960s Rock	$16.99
00702270	1970s Rock	$24.99
00702269	1980s Rock	$16.99

00702268	1990s Rock	$24.99
00369043	Rock Songs for Kids	$14.99
00109725	Once	$14.99
00702187	Selections from O Brother Where Art Thou?	$19.99
00702178	100 Songs for Kids	$16.99
00702515	Pirates of the Caribbean	$17.99
00702125	Praise and Worship for Guitar	$14.99
00287930	Songs from *A Star Is Born, The Greatest Showman, La La Land,* and More Movie Musicals	$16.99
00702285	Southern Rock Hits	$12.99
00156420	Star Wars Music	$16.99
00121535	30 Easy Celtic Guitar Solos	$16.99
00244654	Top Hits of 2017	$14.99
00283786	Top Hits of 2018	$14.99
00302269	Top Hits of 2019	$14.99
00355779	Top Hits of 2020	$14.99
00374083	Top Hits of 2021	$16.99
00702294	Top Worship Hits	$17.99
00702255	VH1's 100 Greatest Hard Rock Songs	$34.99
00702175	VH1's 100 Greatest Songs of Rock and Roll	$34.99
00702253	Wicked	$12.99

ARTIST COLLECTIONS

00702267	AC/DC for Easy Guitar	$16.99
00156221	Adele – 25	$16.99
00396889	Adele – 30	$19.99
00702040	Best of the Allman Brothers	$16.99
00702865	J.S. Bach for Easy Guitar	$15.99
00702169	Best of The Beach Boys	$16.99
00702292	The Beatles — 1	$22.99
00125796	Best of Chuck Berry	$16.99
00702201	The Essential Black Sabbath	$15.99
00702250	blink-182 — Greatest Hits	$17.99
02501615	Zac Brown Band — The Foundation	$17.99
02501621	Zac Brown Band — You Get What You Give	$16.99
00702043	Best of Johnny Cash	$17.99
00702090	Eric Clapton's Best	$16.99
00702086	Eric Clapton — from the Album Unplugged	$17.99
00702202	The Essential Eric Clapton	$17.99
00702053	Best of Patsy Cline	$17.99
00222697	Very Best of Coldplay – 2nd Edition	$17.99
00702229	The Very Best of Creedence Clearwater Revival	$16.99
00702145	Best of Jim Croce	$16.99
00702278	Crosby, Stills & Nash	$12.99
14042809	Bob Dylan	$15.99
00702276	Fleetwood Mac — Easy Guitar Collection	$17.99
00139462	The Very Best of Grateful Dead	$16.99
00702136	Best of Merle Haggard	$16.99
00702227	Jimi Hendrix — Smash Hits	$19.99
00702288	Best of Hillsong United	$12.99
00702236	Best of Antonio Carlos Jobim	$15.99

00702245	Elton John — Greatest Hits 1970–2002	$19.99
00129855	Jack Johnson	$17.99
00702204	Robert Johnson	$16.99
00702234	Selections from Toby Keith — 35 Biggest Hits	$12.95
00702003	Kiss	$16.99
00702216	Lynyrd Skynyrd	$17.99
00702182	The Essential Bob Marley	$16.99
00146081	Maroon 5	$14.99
00121925	Bruno Mars – Unorthodox Jukebox	$12.99
00702248	Paul McCartney — All the Best	$14.99
00125484	The Best of MercyMe	$12.99
00702209	Steve Miller Band — Young Hearts (Greatest Hits)	$12.95
00124167	Jason Mraz	$15.99
00702096	Best of Nirvana	$16.99
00702211	The Offspring — Greatest Hits	$17.99
00138026	One Direction	$17.99
00702030	Best of Roy Orbison	$17.99
00702144	Best of Ozzy Osbourne	$14.99
00702279	Tom Petty	$17.99
00102911	Pink Floyd	$17.99
00702139	Elvis Country Favorites	$19.99
00702293	The Very Best of Prince	$19.99
00699415	Best of Queen for Guitar	$16.99
00109279	Best of R.E.M.	$14.99
00702208	Red Hot Chili Peppers — Greatest Hits	$17.99
00198960	The Rolling Stones	$17.99
00174793	The Very Best of Santana	$16.99
00702196	Best of Bob Seger	$16.99
00146046	Ed Sheeran	$17.99

00702252	Frank Sinatra — Nothing But the Best	$12.99
00702010	Best of Rod Stewart	$17.99
00702049	Best of George Strait	$17.99
00702259	Taylor Swift for Easy Guitar	$15.99
00359800	Taylor Swift – Easy Guitar Anthology	$24.99
00702260	Taylor Swift — Fearless	$14.99
00139727	Taylor Swift — 1989	$19.99
00115960	Taylor Swift — Red	$16.99
00253667	Taylor Swift — Reputation	$17.99
00702290	Taylor Swift — Speak Now	$16.99
00232849	Chris Tomlin Collection – 2nd Edition	$14.99
00702226	Chris Tomlin — See the Morning	$12.95
00148643	Train	$14.99
00702427	U2 — 18 Singles	$19.99
00702108	Best of Stevie Ray Vaughan	$17.99
00279005	The Who	$14.99
00702123	Best of Hank Williams	$15.99
00194548	Best of John Williams	$14.99
00702228	Neil Young — Greatest Hits	$17.99
00119133	Neil Young — Harvest	$14.99

Prices, contents and availability
subject to change without notice.

Visit Hal Leonard online at **halleonard.com**